FROM VISION
INTO REALITY
Talk And Act

Pastor Elijah Smith & Joshua Smith

Order this book online at www.trafford.com
or email orders@trafford.com

Most Trafford titles are also available at major online book retailers.

Printed in the United States of America.

ISBN: 978-1-4907-2970-1 (sc)
ISBN: 978-1-4907-2972-5 (hc)
ISBN: 978-1-4907-2971-8 (e)

Library of Congress Control Number: 2014904274

Trafford rev. 03/10/2014

 www.trafford.com

North America & international
toll-free: 1 888 232 4444 (USA & Canada)
fax: 812 355 4082

Contents

Chapter One

Kanu

Nwankwo Kanu is one of my favourite players who knows how good he would of been he could of been the best player ever if he hadn't had heart problems he has a amazing touch and at sixteen a pios I feel to be so tall and have such a great touch is hard Dimitar Berbatov and Zlatan Ibrahimivic are all alike you couldn't seperate these players Berbatov winning Arsenal the league in 2014 showed his quality similar to Eric Cantana he'll go to Arsenal after Monaco I don't believe any two players are the same but similar yes Kanu was so good and he loved God as well like Didier Diogba who also was great at what he did also Hernandez of Manchester United to clarify Arsenal will win league in May 2014 but Berbatov will be at Monaco then the season later will go and sign for Arsenal but Liverpool in May 2015 will win league Samaras will sign at some point for Hull city keeping them up his style is like Dimitar and Zlatan but a step below Celtic have a big chance to go unbeaten in the season in Scotland

Chapter Two

David Bamford

There were nine or ten players that were far better players than me but David Bamford was on his own with his ability when I Joshua was at Juniour School Holy Spirit there was Lloyd Richardson who ended up playing for England school boys he was exceptional but David Bamford was on a different level David Bamford played for Manchester United Under 21 Danny Cadermarteri was a step below Lloyd Richardson but he truly stood out Bradley Harris and Jay Sobers and Curtis Bernard were on the same level as Danny Cadermarteri other players such as Adam Goldthorpe Andrew Dodsworth and David Thomas were special players along with Stefan I played with Lloyd Richardson at Holy Spirit School he was two years older than Joshua but I played in same school team David Bamford I played in Manchester United Under 21 for one game with him I played with Jay Sobers and Bradley Harris for a game and they were great at Yorkshire Amateurs Academy I played with Stefan and Curtis Bernard at Barnsley James Stansfield was another who I saw as a special player Adam Astle and Christopher Smith and Dean Carter were very good footballers I Joshua played half a game with David Bamford at Carrington he was the best player I've ever seen I saw one half a football from David Bamford which was amazing but in a vision I saw how amazing he was and he did poetry

Chapter Three

Forgiveness

Forgiveness is greater than vengence compassion is more powerfull than anger thats what pastor Elijah has always preached for over fourty years as Christians of no denomination while Danny Cadermarteri and David Thomas and Wesley Milnes and little Nicky were wrong with what they did with my mother and pastor Elijahs wife along with Stephen Slater and Jason Williams how they and others disrespected me showing them the love of Jesus which I have and me Joshua and Pastor Elijah have forgiven them for hate shall not prevail as for Christians doing the same wrong such as Benny Hinn I forgive them as does Pastor Elijah my dad Adam Astle who was a very good footballer as much as he's done wrong he came to visit me in Dewsbury Hospital Dean Carter another who's done wrong but his brother Glenn is a nice man Dean was suppose to be a great player when young but I never saw him play

Dalwinda Singh and Interkaab Razaaq did Joshua wrong as did Christopher Smith but at one point they were Joshua best friends but as soon as Joshua stopped putting himself down they stopped ringing only Stephen Slater continued to ring Jason Williams known as Supa Dupa Lp of 32 Bayswater Terrace Harehills Leeds Stephen Slater lives 209 Snydale Road, Cudworth Barnsley South Yorkshire 572 8EX

Chapter Four

Chinese
and
Arabs

I Joshua enjoy planes the noise the sound it makes when they fly above our house I don't know why but I love it planes are always flying above our house I celebrate with a plane thats why

The Chinese have come into England a few times the Arabs bought the country but the Chinese will take it in 2015

English people will become slaves as I prophesied years ago 2015 is a big year

Chapter Five

About Joshua Life

I Joshua love my brother Elijah and my sisters Collette and Jemima and Catrin and my other brother Paul I love my mum Audrine who I respect she's ill but she's achieved great things and was a general nurse

I love my niece Camille and all my other relatives too much to mention

I love my Dad loads God constantly speaks to me I have had a great life one I would of picked for myself I Joshua speak over seven languages fluently

I promised God I wouldn't touch a woman and devote my life to him something my family never understood they thought I was homosexual I Joshua fell in love with a girl nicknamed Bin Lid in 1998 and at sixteen read about Katie best and promised God I'd love her and take care of her to the very end my first real love Katie best

I'll end by saying Lally respect to all races in another language love you all with the love of Jesus at Yorkshire Amateurs I went in 2003 but the manager Malcolm didn't play non whites I trained with them but didn't play a game at thirty five me Joshua and Elijah and Zara and Katie die we get martyred I Joshua can produce beats I'm a music producer as well as a DJ I did a music technology course and radio course which I both passed

Chapter Six

About Pastor Elijah Life

Pastor Elijah has dementia now but God will heal him he's been a pastor for fourty years he loves God and loves people he has plenty of compassion for people Pastor Elijah speaks some languages fluently Pastor Elijah has a Chinese mother plus coolie in the family back relatives were Scottish his Grandad was Scottish his dad was called David and his mother called Jemima Pastor Elijah is proud to come from Jamaica the West Indies he loves his own country and misses it daily but knows he will go back there soon for thats what God has shown him he plays the trumpet and draws and enjoys writing poems and songs hymns he loves all his children Jemima, Collette, Joshua, Catrin, and Paul

Many are colourbar but Pastor Elijah loves everyone equally Asian, Hispanic, Coolie, Aberijini, everyone from all four corners of the world he loves but preaches what God has told him nothing less he loves people from the United Kingdom and sent messages to the Queen twenty thirty years ago

Chapter Seven

Prophesy From Joshua

I Joshua will play with Elijah my brother for Liverpool and score goals both of us at old Trafford against Manchester United breaking records and winning the league for Liverpool in 2015

They will try and bring Wesley Milnes in through spite for the following season but I Joshua and Elijah won't be here for we'll die at thirty five as martyrs we won't die on a pitch we'll get killed

Me Joshua and Elijah will become famous when we die and just before in 2015

They won't be able to bring in Cadermarteri because he'll be injured or retired

God will heal me of diabetes and my mentle illness mental illness

My niece Camille will do great things for God Collettes children will help Camille after I and Elijah go in 2015

Stan Collymore will win a hundred and one major trophies as manager and three or four champions league trophies at Arsenal he will have great success Clarence Seedorf will also win a hundred and one major trophies as manager with five champions league trophies

Chapter Eight

Prophesy from Pastor Elijah Smith

Elijah won't keep any health in England till he goes back to Jamaica

Blood shed will flow in this country England like a river

Chapter Nine

Joshua Rhyme

I Joshua write my own lyrics

Today is a worry tomorrow is a mystery yesterday is a memory I wrote between 1999 and 2001 I forgive Stephen Slater for trying to take it I truly do love him with the love of Jesus I have rhymed three or seven times with orange heres three Assange and Solange and Zaranj and one more mange I Joshua said in a dedication Stephen taught me today is a worry yesterday a memory tomorrow is a mystery but what I wanted to say is he makes me see that more and more each day I didn't word it but I love him all the same

I've done plenty of poems over three thousand I did gospel music under three names me comely and lyrical gospel and Swift J and put out music on vinyl and put out cds but the producers as good as they were they wasn't sure about me trying to make me come across rubbish but my lyrics were always strong

I use to perform in clubs such as club non in Huddersfield untill God touched me and I stopped doing it in nightclubs I could produce music and I could DJ also

Chapter Ten

Pastor Elijah hymns

Sing a hymn to our Lord

Sing out rejoice Jesus is Lord
our Christ an saviour
let holy hands sing Jesus is Lord
lets raise our hands to give
God the glory a mighty praise
to the almighty
praise our soul the King of heaven
tribute we bring to our mighty King
exalt father God who tends
and spares us to the father son
and holy spirit praise them forever and
ever angels help us to adore him
to him we'll see face to face
even sun bows down before him
lets make sure we are without sin
when we die so that God will
receive our spirit
you can lead a person to knowledge
but you can't make them think

You Jehovah gave me everything

you are my Lord my helper
and redeemer from a child
when I was wild in Jamaica
I loved Jehovah and after
now I'm old the story of Jesus is told
you gave me a wife and that gave me life
    you told me I'd come to England
    and wouldn't keep health in that land
you said it would be like a stones throw
before coming back to Jamaica Land
Isaac or Hezekiah you Jehovah
called me Elijah and also pastor
you gave me a son you named
    that one you gave me two
daughters and my life isn't over
I praise you night and day
I am in constant fellowship
with you Lord and I will when I go back
abroad ascend to heaven will I
will I never die in my seventies or eighties
I am but it says I'm in nineties

A bishop a deacon wether
English or Jamaican
A pastor or Reverend
Wether Scottish or England
no titles taken to
the cross God is boss
We come as simple shepherds
Sometimes we are hazards
bring everything to you

middle day or afternoon or noon
  I know your coming soon
As I born out of my
mothers womb
Jesus came out of the tomb
We love you Lord please
don't bring us into slavery
punish the wicked
and let the saints of God
escape and get free
those that pretend to be Godly
punish them

born round ya
In a Jamaica Kingston or country
going home soon to meet
  my maker for there
  can be only one creater
  nothing can compare
  As God is truly fair

Chapter Eleven

Poems

Katie best

promised God I'd devote my life to him and wouldn't have a woman and fornicate and sin then I read a piece in the sun on the best Katie in the paper it was a sad story and I prayed to God and said with what I read kept it near me at the side of the bed promised God if you give her to me I'd look after her and marry her she'd been in prostitution the story was so sad it got my attention now she always gets a mention she had schizophrenia you'd have to accept that after reading her story it was something to expect look I'm ill with the same diagnosis well Katie we both agree we could never be was she turned from a he into a she by no fault of her own so family did disown was she on coronation street as a boy brown with so much joy well I know what nearly happened to me I nearly ended up getting turned into a girl to next been a lady so much of Katie reminded me of my mummy how she would clap so appealing how she would snap disappointing loved everything about her it was love at first sight from seeing her in the paper to meeting brought great delight she's a prophetess to be a queen but first a princess Gods been great he gives those that love him nothing less than the best

Who would of ever thought it Marilyn Munroe the hottest woman to come on earth one would come greater who was in a league of her own but Katie best is two leagues above her all alone I sometimes take medicine herb like ladies lady like right a girly girl who can play football and doesn't burp when making love you either like it fast or slow I like it slow to begin with but it must end up fast and furious so now you know no need to stay curious

blondes

if a brunette is attractive and pretty
thats better than a average blonde
natural beauty is good
look anyone can go blonde and look good
the key is to see how they look
when there brunettes

Ali Daei

From Iran Gods gifts can go in any person
woman or man scored a hundred
and nine this has to go in rhyme
in a hundred and fourty nine games
Hussein Saeed no where near it
Adnan Al Talyani no where near it
We all need our heroes
no matter what race creed or religion
I'm a Christian who loves Jesus
but I understand this that you can't miss
Ali isn't the best ever but Ferenc Puskas
had eighty four goals in eighty five games
that record stood for years
So to say he scores against rubbish
teams wouldn't be fair
let me make myself clear
a argument goes out that
his gift Ali is rare
football take note
middle east and Asia are here

Usain bolt

How can you say who's the greatest
Sportsman or woman of all time
Pele, Maradonna, George best an the rest
Usain bolt breaking all types of records
fastest man in the world in 2014
how long for like Maurice Greene before
Ronnie O'Sullivan the best snooker player
of all time theres different styles
like Steve Davis on Stephen Hendry
each could claim they were the best
but who will come next pany thats water in hindi
Usain bolt a fellow Jamaican I speak over seven languages
I speak Yardey a legend of the occasion
Steffi Graf an Serena Williams
We love to say who's the best
but its not as simple as contest
you have levels who's in the top three or four
put them to the test Floyd Mayweather
Mohammed Ali
Who else is a legend lately
Iran have Ali Daei I love Christian Benteke
and Hernandez their Godly along with Nwanku Kanu
And Didier Drogba this much is true
As a shadow goes with a dvd Solomon out of my
parents room just like zoom

Chapter Twelve

Wayne Rooney

Wayne Rooney is a good player great I'm not so sure he's a playmaker but a average one and a average goalscorer he probably won't score at 2014 World Cup and will be overweight if he was to play in another World Cup at thirty he'll be nearly finished

Wayne Rooney is a agressive man as he showed after he scored against West ham at Upton Park in Zoll sometimes we just don't comprehend like Sir Alex Ferguson saying cricket and thats it for me love is better than hate the love of Jesus

David Bamford was flat footed his feet I don't know but if that gives you extreme balance because I am flat footed he was more than me

David Bamford was a far greater player than Wayne Rooney I've been to watch Rooney a few times when I saw him I could see Bamford was so far greater Joyce Meyer once said your gift can take you where your character can't keep you so some players have to go down in order to go back up as George Cassey once said

When I play at old Trafford for Liverpool Wayne will make me fall over and Elijah will pick me up Wayne despises me Gods shown me how he thinks about me but I must show love peace and humbleness amongst him as it is very important not to let emotions run wild

Chapter Thirteen

Joshua on football his football

Theres a few players that could get a mention in this book such as Paul Cheetham who was amazing at passing but if that wasn't on song then he had nothing else

I've played at various clubs Howdon Clough Birstall St Patricks, Priestleys, Barnsley, SC Cowersley, Bradford Park Avenue, Liversedge, Tadcaster, Dudley, Layeze Golcar, Wyke, Garforth Town, Thornhill Lees Ossett Town Academy, Yorkshire Amateurs Academy, Garforth Town Academy and many more teams

The teams I trialed for Barnsley Youth U18s Halifax Town, Rochdale, Morecambe and Manchester United Under 21

On each trial I proved myself on the Morecambe one in may 2000 I was unfit but did enough showed enough I even went to David Hunts Soccer Trials but didn't get anywhere at fifteen I went to Nike Soccer Skills and won I went a year later because I wanted to win a bag due to the one I won the zip bust so I went again at sixteen and Ronnie Glavin said to me can I give it to someone else so he gave it to Danny Clapham who was good at goalscoring but lacked a lot Christopher Smith and Christopher Towell came in 1995 and 1996 at seven years old playing football was it makes you wonder about these scouts frazer who was also his age was a good player but Lloyd was far better

I always started off in B teams which I liked because then I had to prove myself which I always did I played a free role at Holy Spirit and on the wing and at the back

I could play most positions effectively I got asked to play for a Sunday team numerous times plus rugby which I said no for I was fairly quick but my sister Collette was quicker

In fact she was quicker than Lloyd Richardson she could of been a athlete

I the end at Twelve I played for Birstall St Patricks U13 I started of in B side played one game at the end of the year season I got spotted by Ipswich Town that season I played centre back at the end of the season I was playing centre forward George was the scout I don't know if he ever rung because I was rarely ever in he did say he was looking for someone older but 1993/94 came and I was striker I scored about fourty goals and a Barnsley Scout called Des came this was after I spoke to a Barnsley fan called Fred I told him about Ipswich so he said we need

Chapter Fourteen

Dewsbury hospital and Emsdale

There so much going on at hospital Sophie at Dewsbury hospital was amazing she was my favourite nurse there were other nurses that were okay but some that were not so good I'm not going to mention them at Emsdale in Halifax it was the same David Bamford we would meet again I nearly frightened him because he had a house warming party and God told me we never spoke about it and I mentioned it and then I told him he told me which he didn't

David had a lust problem which was a problem for he was sleeping with the patients there was a Pakastani girl called Sobia and I see why God sent me there what they were doing to the patients there I couldn't begin to describe it was unbelievable there was another guy who played at Manchester United U21 called Shaun who also was a nurse there who also had a lust problem he knew I know things before they happened so he came into my room and said I'll tell the truth you haven't changed Joshua see more by name see more by nature I respected Shaun not for the wrong he was doing

A poem to Kanu

A truly gifted footballer full of skill he's at top of the bill and plenty ability a heart problem otherwise he may well of been the best player the worlds ever seen I have had a dream he should believe in God for he's been good to him and spared him from sin played at Ajax and Intermilan then he had heart problems went to Arsenal and was like a box of tricks in a parcel then he later went to Portsmouth and God let him win the FA Cup as he did for Didier Drogba both have won the champions league cut down in his peak

Hernandez of Manchester United will break Mexico all time goalscoring record Lukaku will break Belgiums goal record Hernandez loves the Lord

Who knows how good Kanu would of been but at least he played football on the big scene he's a Nigerian who loves Jesus and God made him famous he lived the dream like Roger Milla what they did in adversity was more than handy like Kaka he was great and lively

When I was a young lad I use to call everybody old lad well I was born in Dewsbury

When I was born Audrine my mother saw heavens door open God had spoken my Dad got told he would have a son and he should give me the names he gave me and now we both do poetry and philosophy

About the Authors

Pastor Elijah Smith worked at International Harvester for years and Hipperd and Grinedge before coming a pastor which he has never been paid for he was called by God

Joshua Smith is a servent of the Lord

Joshua has featured in over a hundred poetry Anthologies

Other Books that they have done

It seems all a dream but heres the vision

Authors Pastor Elijah Smith & Joshua Smith